This book is dedicated to all who find Nature not an adversary to conquer and destroy, but a storehouse of infinite knowledge and experience linking man to all things past and present. They know conserving the natural environment is essential to our future well-being.

HAWAI'I VOLCANOES
THE STORY BEHIND THE SCENERY®

by Janet L. Babb

Janet L. Babb, a geologist, leads guided hikes and tours on Kīlauea through her business, Hawaii Volcano GeoVentures. She also conducts Project LAVA (Learning About Volcanic Activity), a workshop for teachers, in cooperation with Hawai'i Volcanoes National Park, and does volunteer work for the U.S.G.S. Hawaiian Volcano Observatory.

Hawai'i Volcanoes National Park *was established in 1916 on the island of Hawai'i to protect the geologic, biologic, and cultural resources on Kīlauea and Mauna Loa, Hawai'i's two most active volcanoes.*

Front cover: Lava lake inside of Pu'u 'Ō'ō vent, photo by G. Brad Lewis. Inside front cover: 'I'iwi feeding on 'ōhi'a lehua nectar; Page 1: Endangered nēnē (Hawaiian geese); photos by Jack Jeffrey.
Page 2/3: Mauna Ulu eruption, NPS photo.

Edited by Cheri C. Madison. Book design by K. C. DenDooven.

Ninth Printing • Revised Edition, 1999

HAWAI'I VOLCANOES: THE STORY BEHIND THE SCENERY. © 1999 KC PUBLICATIONS, INC.
"The Story Behind the Scenery"; "in pictures... The Continuing Story"; the parallelogram forms and colors within are registered in the U.S. Patent and Trademark Office.
LC 98-066948. ISBN 0-88714-143-9.

*I*ncandescent lava, spewed skyward by hissing
   jets of sulfurous gas, destroys everything
in its path. Native plants and animals reclaim barren,
   black volcanic rock, creating a new forest.
      This is the story of Hawai'i Volcanoes—
   an ever-changing, dynamic landscape.

Fountains of fire...raging rivers of red-hot lava... Such volcanic fanfare is not uncommon in Hawai'i Volcanoes National Park, where Kīlauea, home of *Pele*, Hawai'i's goddess of fire, erupts on a regular basis. Kīlauea, one of the most active volcanoes in the world, has erupted nearly 50 times in the past 100 years, treating lucky spectators to fiery displays of molten lava. Although most park visitors witness less dramatic activity, Kīlauea is an awe-inspiring volcano, even as it "sleeps" between eruptions.

From the moment you first peer into Kīlauea's gaping summit crater, the austere beauty of the volcano engages your senses. You see unexpected colors and textures in the stark volcanic landscape, smell pungent gases that seep to the surface from molten rock below, and feel the scalding heat of steam rising from ground cracks. These features are vivid reminders of the ever-present power within Kīlauea Volcano—an immense force waiting to be unleashed.

Active lava flows distinguish this park from all others, but the uniqueness of Hawai'i Volcanoes is not limited to eruptions. The park is well-known for its diverse biological resources, many of which are rare or endangered. Within

A river of lava erupts from an active vent on Kīlauea.

park boundaries, protected forests are home to native birds on the brink of extinction and plants found nowhere else in the world—the last vestige of Hawai'i as it was before humans arrived.

Evidence of Hawai'i's rich cultural heritage is also preserved within the park. Petroglyphs (rock carvings) and ancient trails record the legacy of early Hawaiians who inhabited the slopes of Kīlauea and Mauna Loa. Their respect for the *'āina* (earth) and keen understanding of the volcanoes are expressed in legends of Pele, *ka wahine 'ai honua*, the woman who eats the land.

In Hawai'i Volcanoes National Park, the only constant is change. The landscape you see today did not exist 200 years ago, nor will it exist 200 years from now. The volcanoes erupt, burying acres of forest beneath barren, black rock. Tiny ferns sprout on volcanic rock, giving birth to a new forest. The ongoing struggle between creative and destructive forces continually changes the volcanic landscape. Whether these forces are attributed to Pele or to a strictly scientific interpretation of earth dynamics, the power and beauty of Hawai'i's volcanoes humble the human spirit.

The Volcanoes

Kīlauea is one of two volcanoes in Hawai'i Volcanoes National Park. The other is Mauna Loa, the largest volcano on Earth. Rising 13,679 feet above sea level, Mauna Loa towers over Kīlauea. The base of each volcano rests on the Pacific Ocean floor, so both mountains are even more massive than they appear. From sea floor to summit, Mauna Loa is more than 30,000 feet high—taller than Mt. Everest! Kīlauea rises 4,000 feet above the ocean, but including its submerged foundation, it is at least 20,000 feet high—small compared to Mauna Loa, but a huge volcano nevertheless.

Kīlauea and Mauna Loa grew to their respective heights by erupting repeatedly over several hundred thousand years, with flow upon flow of fluid lava piling up to build broad, gently-sloped mountains. Both volcanoes are still growing—with each eruption adding a new layer of lava to the already impressive pile of rock.

Because their slopes resemble the curved shape of a warrior's shield, Kīlauea and Mauna Loa are called *shield* volcanoes. Park visitors expecting steep-sided cones, like Mount St. Helens or Mt. Fuji, are surprised by Hawai'i's low-profile volcanoes. Kīlauea's summit is so broad and flat that people often don't realize that they are on top of the volcano.

To understand how and why Kīlauea and Mauna Loa erupt, we must look at their relationship to volcanic activity around the world.

Scuba divers film the formation of pillow lava during an underwater eruption. When hot spot magma erupts on the Pacific Ocean floor, seawater quickly cools the red-hot lava, forming a glassy outer skin on the flow. As molten rock inside the flow breaks through the thin crust, it squeezes out like toothpaste, creating irregular lobes that resemble pillows. Every Hawaiian volcano begins with submarine eruptions, so the submerged foundations of Kīlauea and Mauna Loa are composed largely of pillow lavas.

Mauna Loa looms over Kīlauea and the community of Volcano. Mauna Loa, which means "long mountain," is aptly named. With its long, gradual slopes, it is world-famous as a classic shield volcano. Kīlauea's summit caldera and Halema'uma'u Crater are visible on the southeastern flank of Mauna Loa (left). What appears to be a broad plain is actually the top of Kīlauea, a growing shield volcano buttressed against the slopes of its giant neighbor. Hualālai is visible in the far distance (upper right).

PLATES AND HOT SPOTS

According to the theory of global dynamics called *plate tectonics*, the rigid outer layer of Earth is broken into irregular sections called *plates*, which fit together like pieces of a jigsaw puzzle. These rigid plates are in constant motion, "floating" on top of partially molten rock in the Earth's mantle.

When two plates pull away from each other, a gap develops between them, which is filled by *magma* (molten rock beneath the earth's surface). Where plates move toward each other and collide, old crust is destroyed as it is forced back into the mantle, where it remelts. In both cases, whether the plates move apart or collide, magma rises to the surface along the edge of the plate, causing volcanic eruptions.

About 95 percent of the world's 1,500 active volcanoes are located on plate margins. The "ring of fire" that circles the Pacific plate is so named because of frequent eruptions that occur along its boundary. Mount St. Helens in North America, Unzen in Japan, and Pinatubo in the Philippines are notorious ring of fire volcanoes that exploded to life late in the 20th century.

Hawai'i's volcanoes, located in the middle of the Pacific plate 2,500 miles from the nearest plate margin, are not related to volcanic activity at plate boundaries. Instead, they are *hot spot* volcanoes. Heat from a relatively stationary hot spot deep within the Earth melts mantle rock, producing magma that rises through the overlying Pacific plate and erupts on the ocean floor. After thousands of eruptions, an island emerges as *lava* (magma erupted at the earth's surface) builds a rocky mass above sea level. Continuous circulation of molten rock in the mantle replaces the material erupted, so a void does not open up beneath the island.

The Pacific plate is currently drifting to the northwest about four inches each year, carrying older volcanoes away from the hot spot—as if on a conveyor belt—with new volcanoes erupting in place of the old ones. Age dates of the oldest, and now submerged, volcanoes at the north end of the Emperor Seamounts indicate that the hot spot has been active for at least 70 million years. The chain of volcanic islands and atolls that we call the Hawaiian Archipelago trace the Pacific plate's path over the hot spot during the past 40 million years. The Hawaiian Islands lie at the active end of this chain and grow progressively younger to the southeast.

Hawai'i Island, also known as the Big Island, is the youngest in the chain and is presently closest to the hot spot. During the past 750,000 years, the hot spot fueled eruptions on five volcanoes that eventually grew together to form the island. Kohala and Mauna Kea volcanoes have been dormant for thousands of years. Hualālai last erupted in 1801 and may someday erupt again. Mauna Loa and Kīlauea, the youngest and most active of the five volcanoes, have long histories of frequent eruptions that continue to shape the island.

The hot spot also feeds magma to an even younger volcano, Lō'ihi, which lies 20 miles southeast of the Big Island and 3,000 feet below sea level. At that depth, evidence of Lō'ihi's sub-

A cut-away view of Kīlauea reveals the internal "plumbing system" of the volcano. Magma generated by the hot spot moves upward to within a few miles of Kīlauea's summit, where it is stored temporarily. This shallow reservoir consists of interconnected pockets of molten rock. As magma fills the reservoir, the summit of the volcano inflates (swells), a change that can be measured by scientists at the Hawaiian Volcano Observatory and used to predict eruptions. When Kīlauea erupts, magma either rises to the surface and breaks out at the summit of the volcano, or it migrates laterally along zones of weakness within the volcano and breaks out on one of two rift zones, often as a fissure eruption. The movement of magma through the plumbing system causes earthquakes, which are also used to monitor Kīlauea's eruptive activity.

Halema'uma'u, a gaping crater within Kīlauea's summit caldera, is nearly 300 feet deep and 3,000 feet in diameter. The smell of sulfur permeates the air around Halema'uma'u, where tons of volcanic gases leak to the surface every day, encrusting the crater walls with yellow sulfur crystals and converting the rock to light-colored clay minerals.

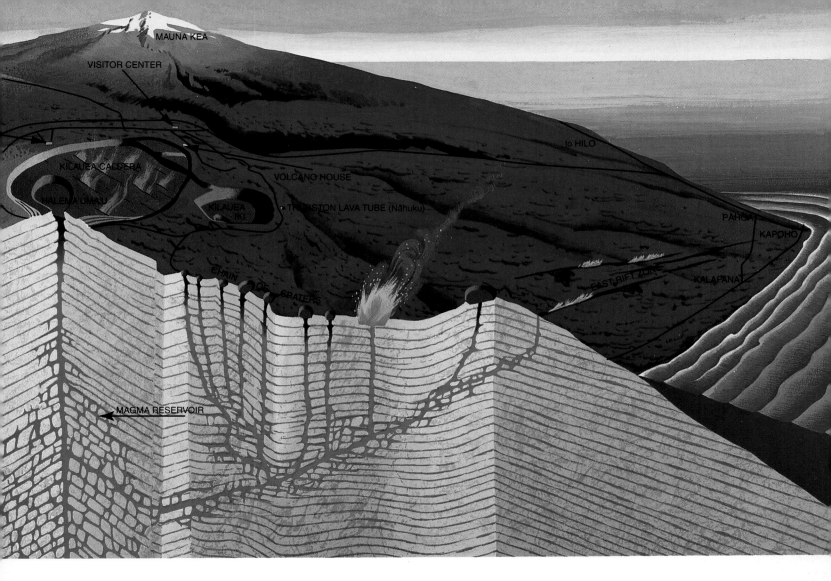

marine eruptions is not visible on the Pacific Ocean surface. If eruptions continue at Lō'ihi, the volcano may one day emerge as Hawai'i's newest island—but don't count on seeing this new Hawaiian real estate for at least 10,000 years.

CALDERAS AND RIFT ZONES

As a shield volcano grows, the top of it commonly collapses to form a summit *caldera* (a depression with steep walls). Some people call this feature a *crater*. To geologists, however, calderas and craters differ in size and origin. A caldera is larger than a crater, and forms by collapse. Craters can form by collapse or by explosion.

The caldera atop Kīlauea is about 3 miles wide and 400 feet deep. Within the caldera, a smaller pit collapsed, forming a crater called Halema'uma'u. Dozens of craters, all created by collapse, also exist on the flanks of Kīlauea, several within view of the appropriately named Chain of Craters Road.

Caldera collapse occurs when huge volumes of molten rock drain from the subsurface reservoir of magma beneath the volcano's summit. Because the top of the volcano is no longer supported by molten rock, it caves in under its own weight.

Once a caldera forms, it slowly refills with lava over hundreds of years, only to collapse again when magma is withdrawn.

When and how Kīlauea's present summit caldera formed has intrigued scientists for decades. Did it collapse in a single catastrophic event? Or was it the final event in a series of smaller collapses that occurred over tens or hundreds of years? Ongoing research may someday provide the answers to these questions.

A caldera known as Moku'āweoweo has been present at the summit of Mauna Loa for the past 1,200 years. While Kīlauea's caldera is easily viewed from overlooks along Crater Rim Drive, the exhilarating view into Moku'āweoweo is reserved for only the hardiest backpackers. There are no roads to the top of Mauna Loa— only rugged hiking trails across harsh, moon-like terrain.

In Hawaiian eruptions, magma rises to the surface either at the top of the volcano or along a *rift zone*, a well-defined zone of weakness that stretches from the summit through the flank of the volcano. All of Hawai'i's volcanoes have one or more rift zones. Kīlauea and Mauna Loa both have two.

Fountains of lava up to 1,780 feet high roared from Kīlauea's east rift zone during the Mauna Ulu eruption. Beginning in May 1969, the eruption continued for over five years. Episodic high fountains produced lava flows that poured into and eventually filled 'Ālo'i and 'Alae craters near the main vent.

Kīlauea seems to alternate between long phases of summit eruptions and long phases of rift zone eruptions. From 1823, when the volcano was first described in writing, to 1934, most of Kīlauea's activity took place at its summit caldera. It was during this period that Mark Twain, in 1866, described the nearly continuous lava lake in Halema'uma'u as "a heaving sea of molten fire." Kīlauea was quiet from 1934 to 1952—no eruptions for 18 years! Since 1955, most of Kīlauea's eruptions have occurred on its east rift zone. Kīlauea's southwest rift zone has been less active, with only two short-lived eruptions (1971 and 1974) in recent decades.

Mauna Loa has erupted more than 30 times in the past 150 years. The eruptions typically begin at the summit of the volcano with *curtains of fire* (lava shooting into the air from long, narrow ground cracks) that later migrate down the volcano's northeast or southwest rift zones. In 1984, during Mauna Loa's most recent eruption, Hilo residents anxiously watched as vents on the northeast rift zone sent lava flows within four miles of the city limits.

FLOW OR BLOW?

Hawai'i's volcanoes are renowned for their relatively benign eruptions. Indeed, Kīlauea has the reputation of being a "drive-in" volcano. When Kīlauea erupts, visitors and island residents converge on the volcano to witness its fiery show—unlike at explosive volcanoes, where people run for their lives during an eruption.

The driving force of all volcanic eruptions is gas. As magma migrates upward, the dissolved gases in it expand, creating enough pressure to push lava to the surface. The "quiet" nature of Hawaiian eruptions is due to the fluidity of hot spot magma. In fluid magma, gases can escape with relative ease and typically do not build pressures to the point of exploding. If magma is *viscous* (thick and pasty)—the kind produced at colliding plate boundaries—gases accumulate and pressure builds within the volcano. The end result is usually a catastrophic explosion, like those that occurred at Mount St. Helens in 1980 and Pinatubo in 1991.

In Hawai'i, jets of escaping gas often propel fluid lava high into the air. Fountains of lava roared from Kīlauea Iki in 1959, reaching heights of 1,900 feet—the highest ever recorded in Hawai'i and possibly the highest on Earth. Those lava fountains looked explosive but were actually much less violent than the eruptions at Mount St. Helens and Pinatubo.

PETER FRENCH

A river of molten rock about 20 feet wide flows downslope of the active vent on Kīlauea's east rift zone. As soon as 2000° F lava is exposed to air, it begins to cool and harden, creating pieces of solid rock that are rafted along on the surface of the flow.

This does not mean that Hawai'i's volcanoes are never dangerous. Explosive eruptions are very much a part of Kīlauea's history. One such event occurred in 1790, when the volcano erupted so violently that magma was blown apart to form ash rather than lava flows. At least 80 Hawaiians were killed by the blast, making it more deadly than Mount St. Helens in 1980. Ash deposits up to 40 feet thick, erupted in 1790 and earlier, can be seen in cliffs and gullies along the southern margin of Kīlauea's summit caldera.

A smaller explosion occurred in 1924, during which the walls of Halema'uma'u were ripped apart, doubling the size of the crater. Blocks of rock, some weighing tons, were blasted thousands of feet from the crater. Rocky debris litters the surface around the crater rim, most of it still lying where it landed more than 70 years ago.

Geologists believe that the 1790 and 1924 events were caused by sudden drainage of a long-lived lava lake in Halema'uma'u. As magma drained from the conduit beneath the lava lake, groundwater seeped in and flashed to steam when it encountered hot rock. This steam created tremendous pressure, which exploded to the surface, hurling rock fragments from the crater and sending clouds of dust more than 20,000 feet into the air.

Although Kīlauea's "quiet" eruptions far outnumber its explosive ones, we should not lose sight of the volcano's potential fury. Numerous ash deposits erupted thousands of years ago have been discovered on Kīlauea, suggesting a long history of violent events. One may not happen in your lifetime, but given Kīlauea's history, future explosive eruptions are to be expected.

JEFFREY JUDD

JANET L. BABB

LAVA FLOWS, TUBES, AND TEARS

Lava erupted from Hawai'i's volcanoes is about 2100° F—ten times hotter than boiling water. As soon as it reaches the Earth's surface, molten rock begins to cool and harden. Lava that solidifies with a smooth, billowy, or ropy surface is called *pāhoehoe*. Flows characterized by a rough, jagged, or rubbly surface are called *'a'ā*. These two terms are Hawaiian words, but they are recognized and used by volcanologists around the world.

Ash layers exposed in cracks and gullies along Kīlauea's southwest rift zone provide evidence of the volcano's violent past. The buff-colored layers, known as the Keanakāko'i Ash, were deposited during explosive eruptions in 1790 and earlier. Magma injected along the southwest rift zone in 1868 caused large ground cracks to open at the surface, exposing the thick ash deposits. In 1971, lava poured into the crack during a five-day fissure eruption, creating a crust of black rock.

Lava gushes from a vent on Kīlauea's east rift zone creating a dome fountain. These relatively low-energy hemispherical fountains occur when a large volume of gas-poor lava is erupted at a nearly constant rate. This lava dome, which occurred during the Mauna Ulu eruption, fountained continuously for hours on October 11, 1969, reaching heights of 60 feet and generating a flood of lava (foreground) that ponded around the active vent.

The rough, jagged surface of this active 'a'ā lava flow (about four feet thick) contrasts sharply with the smooth, billowy surface of pāhoehoe lava beneath it. As 'a'ā lava moves downslope, the crust of the flow is torn into loose, jagged pieces that conceal a massive, dense interior.

This skylight provides a glimpse of molten rock flowing through an active lava tube on Kīlauea Volcano. Skylights form when a section of the tube roof collapses, exposing the subsurface river of lava. The fast-moving lava flows silently beneath the skylight, creating a swirl or eddy as it drops to a lower level in the tube.

Lava tubes develop when the top of a flow crusts over, enclosing a molten stream of lava in a tunnel of hardened rock. The solid crust acts as an insulator, preventing heat loss, so the lava inside the tube remains hot and fluid, and is able to travel long distances from the *vent* (the opening where magma reaches the surface). One of the longest tube-fed flows on the island began at Kīlauea's summit and entered the ocean at Kaloli Point—a distance of 24 miles!

At the end of an eruption, the remaining lava in the tube may drain out almost completely, leaving a cave-like feature. Kīlauea and Mauna Loa are riddled with countless lava tubes, many of which were used by early Hawaiians for shelter and other purposes. Because they contain important geological, biological, and archaeological resources that have not yet been documented, most tubes in the park are closed to the public. An exception is Nāhuku (also known as Thurston Lava Tube), which can be explored by park visitors.

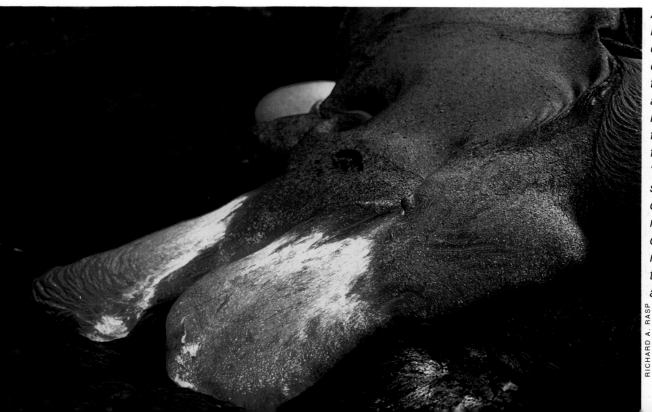

A thin, flexible crust immediately congeals on the surface of lava exposed to air, slowing the leading edge of a pāhoehoe flow. As the molten interior of the flow continues to push forward, incandescent "toes" break through the semi-solid crust, which can fold and twist to form ropy patterns characteristic of pāhoehoe lava. Within moments, the lava turns black as it cools and hardens.

RICHARD A. RASP

JANET L. BABB

Pele's hair, strands of volcanic glass as thin as human hair, glistens in the sunlight. Carried by the wind, this Pele's hair drifted to the Ka'ū Desert where it accumulated against the rocks, forming a mat of golden glass.

Pele's tears, named for Hawai'i's goddess of volcanoes, form as molten rock is blasted skyward in high lava fountains. The fragments of frothy lava quickly cool, creating tiny droplets of black volcanic glass.

Crystals of yellow sulfur encrust the rock around solfataras, vents where sulfur gases seep to the surface of a volcano. The acidic gases alter the surrounding rock, creating deposits of a reddish-brown mineral called hematite.

PHILIP ROSENBERG

JANET L. BABB

In vigorous eruptions, jets of gas propel fluid lava skyward, creating fountains of frothy lava. As red-hot fragments fly through the air, they may cool and solidify, falling to the ground as *cinder*, or they can remain semi-molten, forming *spatter*. During the 1959 Kīlauea Iki eruption, fragments from the high fountains fell around the vent, building a 400-foot-high *cinder and spatter cone* called Pu'u Pua'i, "fountain hill."

Tiny droplets of fluid lava forced upward in a fountain often become streamlined, taking on the shape of a teardrop. The droplets quickly cool to form beads of volcanic glass known as *Pele's tears*. Fine strands of molten lava trailing behind the tears are called *Pele's hair*. These golden threads of volcanic glass, carried by the wind for miles, usually accumulate in folds and cracks of older rock downwind of the vent.

USGS PHOTO

Molten rock pouring into the ocean is chilled so suddenly by seawater that the lava shatters—sometimes explosively—into small glassy particles of black sand. Ocean currents carry the sand downshore, where it may accumulate along the coast creating a black-sand beach, for which Hawai'i is famous.

During Kīlauea's ongoing eruption, sulfur dioxide and other volcanic gases are released from vents on Pu'u 'Ō'ō (a cinder and spatter cone) and the active lava tube (lower right). Sulfur dioxide reacts with sunlight and atmospheric particles to create air pollution known as volcanic smog or vog. Prevailing winds usually blow the vog to the west side of the island, but under calm wind conditions, a gray haze of vog can settle on areas within the park.

A Changing Landscape

More than 90 percent of Kīlauea's surface has been covered by lava flows in the past 1,100 years—no surprise since Kīlauea is Hawai'i's youngest and most active volcano. In the past century alone, several eruptions significantly altered the landscape within Hawai'i Volcanoes National Park. Two such events, the 1924 Halema'uma'u steam explosion and 1959 Kīlauea Iki lava fountains, added a field of boulders and a cinder cone to Kīlauea's summit.

From 1969 to 1974, an eruption on Kīlauea's upper east rift zone covered 18 square miles of forest and grassland with lava and added 210 acres of new land to the island. During the eruption, molten rock piled up around the main vent, building a 400-foot-high mound, or *lava shield*, named Mauna Ulu, a prominent feature still visible in the park today.

Lava flows from Mauna Ulu buried nearly 13 miles of the Chain of Craters Road, which was opened only four years earlier. Lava cascaded over Hōlei Pali, a steep cliff on Kīlauea's south flank, advanced across the coastal plain, and poured into the ocean 7 miles from the vent. These extensive flows, frozen in time as dark-colored rock, can be seen from overlooks along the Chain of Craters Road, reopened in 1979.

In the last 100 years, Mauna Loa has erupted less frequently than Kīlauea. The two most recent eruptions, 1975 and 1984, were short-lived, lasting only one day and three weeks, respectively. But when Mauna Loa comes to life, it makes up for lost time. In less than one *hour*, Mauna Loa can erupt the same volume of molten rock that Kīlauea erupts in one *day*. Torrents of lava gush

One of the most stunning views in Hawai'i Volcanoes is that of Pu'u Pua'i, the 400-foot-high cinder and spatter cone created by lava fountains in 1959. Halema'uma'u Crater and the slope of Mauna Loa are visible in the background.

from the massive volcano, creating large, fast-moving flows that are spectacular—and sometimes frightening.

Prior to the 1975 and 1984 eruptions, Mauna Loa spent more than a year bringing itself back to life, swelling and shaking as magma moved beneath the volcano. Since 1984, Mauna Loa has slowly re-inflated with magma, but is still resting fairly quietly. For now, scientists are waiting and watching for clues to the next eruption, expected in the early 21st century, if not before.

In addition to lava flows, two strong earthquakes altered Kīlauea's landscape in recent time.

Lava flowing through a forest cools and hardens around the trunks of living trees. When the molten interior of the flow drains away, the solid crust of lava surrounding a tree is left standing, forming a column of rock known as a lava tree. Spatter, blobs of molten lava, subsequently piled up on top of this lava tree, giving it an unusual broccoli-like shape.

Submerged palm trees at Halapē are stark reminders of the sudden changes that can occur on an active volcano. Intrusions of magma into Kīlauea's rift zones push the south flank of the volcano toward the sea, resulting in periodic large earthquakes and substantial movements along the coast.

will continue to play an important role in shaping the landscape.

MONITORING HAWAI'I'S VOLCANOES

There is no place on the globe so favorable for systematic study of volcanology and the relations of local earthquakes to volcanoes as in Hawaii...where the earth's primitive processes are at work making new land and adding new gases to the atmosphere.

—THOMAS A. JAGGAR

In 1975, the largest earthquake in over 100 years—magnitude 7.2—rattled the island, causing subsidence along the south flank of Kīlauea. At Halapē, the shoreline dropped more than ten feet, flooding a grove of palm trees and killing two campers. At Kīlauea's summit, a section of Crater Rim Drive collapsed into the caldera. In 1983, a magnitude 6.6 earthquake centered on the Ka'ōiki fault zone between Kīlauea and Mauna Loa, triggered collapse along the caldera rim once again. This collapse took out another large section of Crater Rim Drive, causing the park to permanently re-route the road. The dynamic nature of Hawai'i's volcanoes guarantees that earthquakes

Kīlauea, a relatively safe, easily accessed, and frequently active volcano, has become a mecca for scientists from around the world who want to study volcanic processes in action. Kīlauea's value as a permanent site for scientific observation was recognized by Thomas A. Jaggar, who founded the Hawaiian Volcano Observatory (HVO) in 1912. Today, HVO is operated by the U.S. Geological Survey, with a cadre of scientists monitoring and studying Hawai'i's active volcanoes.

Prior to an eruption, magma migrates upward or laterally within the volcano, slowly

New land created by lava flowing into the ocean is unstable and often collapses without warning, forming sheer cliffs. Shortly after this section of Kīlauea's coast collapsed, molten rock continued to pour from the active lava tube, rebuilding a new "bench" of land and setting the stage for another collapse.

Scientists from the Hawaiian Volcano Observatory routinely collect samples of lava as part of their ongoing research projects and monitoring activities. A sampling tool attached to the end of a steel cable is lowered through a skylight into the river of molten rock inside an active lava tube. When lava adheres to the tool, the cable is quickly—and carefully—pulled out of the tube. Samples are also collected from surface lava flows. Laboratory analyses of the samples are conducted to determine the temperature and chemical composition of the lava, which provide important information about changing conditions within Hawai'i's active volcanoes.

making its way to the surface. This forceful *intrusion* of magma causes the volcano to swell, or *inflate*, and triggers small earthquakes—warning signals of an impending eruption. The main scientific instruments used to track magma movement are seismometers, which can detect the slightest unrest within the volcano, and tiltmeters, which measure subtle changes in its shape.

A network of instruments on Kīlauea and Mauna Loa feed data to the observatory 24 hours a day, 7 days a week. You can enjoy your visit to Hawai'i Volcanoes National Park, knowing that scientists are "minding the volcano." When significant changes occur, HVO is in constant communication with park rangers and public safety officials, who take appropriate action to ensure the safety of visitors and local residents.

The Hawaiian Volcano Observatory (HVO), perched on the rim of Kīlauea's summit caldera, continuously monitors seismic and volcanic activity on Hawai'i Island. The staff of about 25 people includes scientists and technical specialists in seismology, geology, geochemistry, geophysics, ground deformation, computer science, and electronics. Knowledge gained from HVO's research on volcanic processes has been applied to active volcanoes around the world. The observatory is not open to the public, but exhibits in the adjacent Jaggar Museum, operated by the national park, illustrate how HVO scientists monitor and study Hawai'i's volcanoes.

High lava fountains roaring from Pu'u 'Ō'ō, a vent on Kīlauea's east rift zone, created fiery displays that could be seen for miles. Fountains up to 1,500 feet high erupted about once a month for three years (1983-86), covering areas downwind of the vent with a blanket of cinder, pumice, Pele's tears, and Pele's hair.

KĪLAUEA TODAY

Just after midnight on January 3, 1983, following a swarm of small earthquakes, the ground cracked open on the east flank of Kīlauea, near Nāpau Crater in Hawai'i Volcanoes National Park. Within moments, molten rock and sulfurous gases spewed to the surface, lighting the night sky with a spectacular curtain of fire—the first of several fissure eruptions to break out during the next six months.

By June 1983, the eruption settled down to a single vent near the eastern boundary of the park. Over the next three years, lava fountains up to 1,500 feet high roared from the vent 44 times. Although each episode usually lasted less than 24 hours, fallout from the fountains piled up around the vent, building an 835-foot-high cinder and spatter cone called Pu'u 'Ō'ō.

In July 1986, the eruption shifted to a new vent, Kūpaianaha, two miles farther down the rift zone. Instead of episodic high fountaining, fluid lava poured nearly continuously from Kūpaianaha for almost six years. During that time, the eruption captured worldwide attention as voluminous outpourings of lava wreaked havoc on Kīlauea's south flank.

Hardest hit were the coastal communities of Kapa'ahu and Kalapana, entombed beneath 50 to 80 feet of lava by the end of 1990. Flows also inundated the shoreline, burying the famous Kaimū black-sand beach and filling the bay with black rock. In the park, lava flows destroyed the Waha'ula Visitor Center.

Early in 1992, activity at Kūpaianaha ceased, but the eruption resumed almost immediately at vents on the flanks of Pu'u 'Ō'ō. In its march to the sea, lava buried Kamoamoa, an early Hawaiian settlement and a park campground/picnic area.

Pu'u 'Ō'ō, a cinder and spatter cone created by 44 episodes of high lava fountains, reached a maximum height of 835 feet, becoming the highest landmark on Kīlauea's east rift zone. When the eruption shifted to a new vent in 1986, the cone began to slowly crumble.

After years of slowly falling apart, Pu'u 'Ō'ō suffered a major collapse in January 1997. In response to an intrusion west of Pu'u 'Ō'ō, the lava pond inside the cinder cone drained away. No longer supported by molten rock, the crater floor and part of the cone collapsed, creating a huge gap on its west flank. Today, Pu'u 'Ō'ō, which continues to disintegrate, is being slowly buried by lava flows piling up around it.

 STEVE & DONNA O'MEARA/VOLCANO WATCH INTERNATIONAL

Except for brief pauses, lava continues to flow down the slopes of Kīlauea. January 3, 1998, marked the 15th anniversary of Kīlauea's latest eruption—with no indication that the activity will end any time soon.

Lava pouring into the ocean—about 90,000 gallons per minute in recent years—piles up to form rocky ledges in front of old sea cliffs. Because these *benches* are unstable and often collapse with no warning, they are extremely hazardous and strictly off limits. Unfortunately, injuries and loss of life have occurred during this eruption because people failed to obey park warning signs and ventured too close to an active bench.

This eruption has become the longest-lived rift zone eruption in recorded history, and Kīlauea's most destructive event of the 20th century. In one and a half decades, lava covered 38 square miles of public and private land, destroying 181 homes, a church, a store, a community center, a county park, and several national park structures. Eight miles of highway, vast tracts of forest, and thousands of archaeological features were also overrun by molten rock.

Yet in the same 15 years, nearly 600 acres of new land were added to the island, a testament of Kīlauea's creative power. Where lava meets the sea, we can witness the ongoing battle between creation and destruction—a constant conflict to which all life on Hawai'i's active volcanoes must adapt.

SUGGESTED READING

DECKER, ROBERT, and BARBARA DECKER. *Volcanoes*. New York: W. H. Freeman, 1998 (revised edition).

HAZLETT, RICHARD W. *Geological Field Guide, Kīlauea Volcano*. Hawai'i National Park: Hawai'i Natural History Association, 1993.

HELIKER, CHRISTINA, and DORIAN WEISEL. *Kīlauea, The Newest Land on Earth*. Honolulu: Island Heritage Publishing, 1996.

JUVIK, S. T., J. O. JUVIK, and T. R. PARADISE. *Atlas of Hawai'i*. Honolulu: University of Hawai'i Press, 1998.

MACDONALD, GORDON A., and DOUGLASS H. HUBBARD. *Volcanoes of the National Parks in Hawai'i*. Hawai'i National Park: Hawai'i Natural History Association, 1993 (revised edition).

TILLING, ROBERT I., CHRISTINA HELIKER, and THOMAS L. WRIGHT. *Eruptions of Hawaiian Volcanoes: Past, Present and Future*. Denver: U.S. Geological Survey, 1987.

A torrent of molten rock gushes over Paliuli, a low cliff above Kīlauea's coastal plain, in 1994. For years, flow upon flow cascaded over the cliff, encrusting a broad swath of Paliuli with glassy pāhoehoe lava and burying countless archaeological features in the area. The flows often dribbled over Paliuli in narrow, slow-moving streams that created elaborate textures and patterns in the rock. But at times such as this, wide rivers of red-hot lava raged over the cliff.

Following a three-year period of increasing earthquake activity and summit inflation, Mauna Loa erupted on March 25, 1984. The eruption began in Mokuʻāweoweo, the volcano's summit caldera—but within a few hours, the activity shifted to Mauna Loa's northeast rift zone, where a curtain of fire more than a mile long spewed molten rock up to 150 feet into the air. As fountains of lava roared from the vent, red-hot rock piled up on both sides of the active fissure, forming a massive spatter rampart. Erupting at a rate of nearly 9 million gallons per minute, lava flowed down Mauna Loa's north flank at speeds of 300 to 700 feet per hour. By March 29, a river of lava was within four miles of Hilo, but fortunately, the flow stagnated. Mauna Loa continued to erupt for two more weeks, sending other flows toward Hilo, but none reached the city limits before the eruption ended on April 15.

Overleaf: Where lava pours into the ocean, seawater flashes to steam in small explosions, creating "bubbles" of molten lava that shatter into delicate ribbons and thin flakes of volcanic glass. Photo by G. Brad Lewis.

New Life on a New Land

The Hawaiian Islands, thousands of miles from the nearest continent, are among the most isolated land masses on Earth. When the first volcano in the island chain rose above sea level millions of years ago, the vast ocean surrounding it created a daunting barrier to the migration of terrestrial plants and animals. The odds against any living creature reaching the island—a mere speck of rock in the middle of the Pacific Ocean—were staggering. But slowly, perhaps at the rate of only one species every 70,000 years, life found its way to the new land.

Seeds, spores, and insects small enough to be blown aloft were carried to the island by wind. Plant seeds tolerant of saltwater floated on ocean currents and washed ashore. Birds and bats flew to the island, or were blown there by high winds during fierce storms. Like feathered cargo carriers, migrating birds transported seeds across the

Kōlea, *Pacific golden plovers, migrate about 3,000 miles to spend winters in Hawai'i. Before returning to their arctic nesting grounds in late April, males acquire dramatic breeding plumage highlighted by a white stripe.*

Pacific, either in their digestive systems or stuck to their feathers or muddy feet. Insects, spiders, and small snails also hitchhiked to the island by way of birds or drifted across the ocean on rafts of floating debris.

Once life was established on the first island, colonization of subsequent islands was somewhat less arduous. As volcanoes emerged from the ocean one after another, plants and animals migrated down the chain from older to younger islands—a relatively easy trip compared to crossing the Pacific Ocean from the nearest continent, but fraught with hardship nevertheless.

Of the thousands of plants and animals living on continents around the Pacific, very few successfully migrated to the islands. Those that were too heavy to be carried by wind, or unable to fly long distances or withstand saltwater, had no hope of crossing the ocean. Amphibians, terrestrial reptiles, and large land mammals failed to reach the islands until much later—and then only because they were brought by humans.

The excursion across the Pacific was not easy, but thriving on inhospitable, black rock of a still-growing volcanic island was perhaps even more difficult. Some plants and animals lived through the trans-oceanic odyssey only to perish on the islands due to lack of appropriate habitat or their inability to reproduce. To endure, each colonizing species needed a place with the proper climate and enough food and water to support them. Producing viable offspring was an even greater challenge than finding suitable habitat. Many species that reached the islands probably consisted of only one or two individual plants or animals. If those individuals were infertile, or could not find a mate, the species was doomed.

In spite of the odds against them, a thousand or so plant and animal species successfully colonized the islands and began the long process of adapting to their new home. These

The high canopy of this Hawaiian rain forest is dominated by ʻōhiʻa, a member of the myrtle family. These native trees, characterized by hard, dark red wood, can reach heights of 60 to 80 feet. Below the ʻōhiʻa canopy, hāpuʻu tree ferns form a distinct layer that shades the dense forest understory. In the 1800s, tree ferns were cut to harvest pulu (silky fibers that cover young hāpuʻu fronds), which was used to stuff pillows and mattresses.

hardy pioneers were the ancestors of Hawaiʻi's diverse native flora and fauna.

The plants and animals that reached the islands naturally—without human help—are known as *native* or *indigenous* species. Because they evolved on isolated islands, most native species developed over time into unique plants and animals that exist only in Hawaiʻi. These *endemic* species are truly special because they are found nowhere else in the world.

ADAPTING TO THE ISLANDS

Plants and animals that made it to the islands alive found themselves in a strange environment, separated from the flora and fauna of their homelands. The volcanic landscape, although unfamiliar, was a "land of opportunity" for colonizing species. Differences in geology, climate, and elevation created a variety of habitats, ranging from newly-erupted, barren lava flows to ancient, forest-covered slopes; from dry, stark deserts to lush rain forests; from warm, wave-splashed shorelines to frigid, snowcapped mountaintops.

As native plants and animals spread from island to island and from sea level to summit, they utilized the available resources in these various

27

Common 'amakihi *are often seen searching for insects or nectar on small, leafy branches and in the tops of trees in upland forests and woodlands. The flat trilling song of this small, yellowish-green honeycreeper, one of Hawai'i's most common native forest birds, can be heard year-round.*

JACK JEFFREY

pathways not previously possible. Some adaptations ended in failure, but others succeeded, giving rise to numerous and diverse life forms.

No large land mammals initially existed on the islands, so some native plants evolved without thorns, pungent odors, and other protective features needed to discourage grazing and browsing herbivores. "Mintless" mints and nettles without stinging hairs are examples of native plants adapted to a predator-free environment. Unfortunately, when cattle, goats, and other grazers and browsers were later introduced to the islands, Hawai'i's "defenseless" plants suffered huge losses, some to the point of extinction.

By the time the volcanoes of Hawai'i Island emerged from the sea, plants and animals had been evolving in isolation on the islands for more than 20 million years, resulting in a large number of endemic species. Consequently, Hawai'i's native ecosystems are delicately balanced and extremely vulnerable to disturbances.

LIFE VERSUS LAVA

With frequent eruptions of Mauna Loa and Kīlauea, lava flows continually disturb the natural environment in Hawai'i Volcanoes, but life goes on. How soon plants and animals become established on a new lava flow depends on several variables, including elevation, rainfall, distance from seed source, and type of lava flow.

Surprisingly, insects usually colonize new lava before plants do, often within a month of an eruption—even if the flow is still warm. One of the first to arrive is the dark-colored lava flow cricket. These nocturnal insects hide in deep cracks of solidified lava during the day to avoid desiccation and emerge at night to eat windblown debris on the surface of the flow. When plants begin to grow and fill in the cracks and crevices, the crickets must find new homes on younger, unvegetated lava in order to survive.

Algae, one of the first plants to colonize new lava, can start growing on a flow within six months of an eruption. The next plants to arrive include ferns, 'ōhi'a trees, lichens, and mosses, which sprout from tiny seeds and spores blown onto the flow by wind. With the right climate,

habitats to survive. In doing so, most of them experienced changes in their physical appearance and/or behavior as they adapted to their surroundings. Over time, these changes led to the development of new, distinct species. This process of evolution, in which a large number of diverse species evolve from a single ancestral species, is known as *adaptive radiation*.

One of the more remarkable stories of adaptive radiation is that of the Hawaiian honeycreepers. A rather nondescript bird related to house finches evolved on the islands into more than 40 kinds of honeycreepers that vary in size, color, behavior, and song. The most notable difference among honeycreeper species is the size and shape of their beaks. As the birds adapted to island life, some of them grew a thick bill for crushing seeds or twigs, while others developed a delicate bill for feeding on insects, a curved bill for sipping nectar from flowers, or a straight bill for pecking at wood. With their many adaptations, honeycreepers are unequaled in their ability to occupy a wide range of habitats.

Being isolated from related flora and fauna created a genetic dead end for some plants and animals, and led to their extinction. But in one respect, Hawai'i's isolation was an advantage to colonizing species: Most of the competitors, predators, and diseases that threatened life on distant continents did not exist on the islands. Liberated from those threats, native plants and animals were free to embark on evolutionary

The Hawaiian lava flow cricket is known only from unvegetated lava flows of Kīlauea. Discovered in 1973, it appears to be an evolutionary stepping stone between endemic beach crickets and endemic cave (lava tube) crickets, all of which are mute, deaf, and flightless. Lava flow crickets are dark-colored, unlike the light-colored lava tube crickets.

Swordferns, or kupukupu, *are among the first plants to colonize new lava flows. (Kupu means "to sprout.")* Characterized by narrow, feather-shaped fronds, these swordferns are growing where tiny spores, blown in by the wind, took root in shady, damp cracks on solid pāhoehoe lava.

plants can become well-established on a lava flow in only 10 years. Where precipitation is plentiful, mature rain forests can develop in as little as 400 years.

Lava flows generally move downslope in rivers or channels of molten rock that snake their way around higher ground, leaving sections of land untouched. These "islands" of older, vegetated land are called *kīpuka*. The sea of lava surrounding the islands creates a barrier to the invasion of non-native species, so *kīpuka* often contain rich resources of native plants and animals, some of which evolve into endemic species.

Kīpuka of various sizes and ages are scattered throughout Hawai'i Volcanoes. These isolated patches of vegetation are important sources of seeds, spores, and insects that colonize new lava flows. Without them, some native species might be lost forever. One of the last remnants of Hawai'i's ancient forests is preserved in Kīpuka Puaulu (Bird Park). Fortunately, lava flows spared this area when Mauna Loa erupted 400 years ago, so park visitors today can enjoy the experience of walking through 2,000-year-old forest.

The trail in Kīpuka Puaulu leads park visitors through an ancient upland forest that is home to some of the rarest plants and animals in the world. Once subjected to cattle grazing, this kīpuka on the Mauna Loa Road is now fenced to protect its diverse vegetation.

Niu, *or coconut palms, and white sand are not common in Hawai'i Volcanoes, but they do occur at a few remote coastal sites. These geologically older shoreline areas can be reached only by hiking through the hot, dry lowlands of the park.*

PLANT COMMUNITIES

Extending from sea level to nearly 14,000 feet elevation, Hawai'i Volcanoes encompasses seven ecological zones, each of which is characterized by a distinct community of native plants. These zones—*seacoast, lowlands, mid-elevation woodlands, rain forests, upland forests, subalpine,* and *alpine*—are delineated by differences in elevation and rainfall. While some plants are confined to specialized niches, other species have adapted to a wide range of environmental conditions and thrive in more than one zone.

The rocky cliffs, tide pools, and beaches along the seacoast have been subject to change by lava flows in recent years. Native plants in this zone, such as *pōhuehue* (beach morning glory) and *naupaka kahakai*, both of which grow on or near sandy beaches along older shorelines, must be able to withstand salt spray, intense sunshine, and hot, windy conditions.

Park lowlands extend from the seacoast up to an elevation of about 2,000 feet. Bounded on the north by the steep Hilina and Hōlei *pali* (cliffs), this hot, dry zone has been heavily impacted by goat and cattle ranching, as well as by

Unlike native grasses, the alien grasses that have invaded middle and low elevations in the park readily carry fire. Beautiful 'ōhi'a woodlands (background) can be seen along Hilina Pali Road—but during times of drought, the road is closed to prevent accidental wildfire.

fire. Many of the plants growing in the lowlands today were introduced by Polynesian settlers. Extensive areas have also been covered by lava flows during the 20th century. Thus, very little of the original lowland flora has survived.

Mid-elevation woodlands along Kīlauea's upper east rift zone consist of *'ōhi'a* trees and *'iliahi* (sandalwood), a tree that was heavily exploited during the early 19th century for its fragrant wood. Ferns include *uluhe*, a fast-growing and widespread fern that forms nearly impenetrable mats, and *'ama'u*, a large fern for which Halema'uma'u Crater is believed to have been named.

'Apapane, *small Hawaiian honeycreepers, are often seen sipping nectar from* lehua, *the delicate, scarlet-red blossoms on 'ōhi'a trees, or catching insects in the forest canopy.*

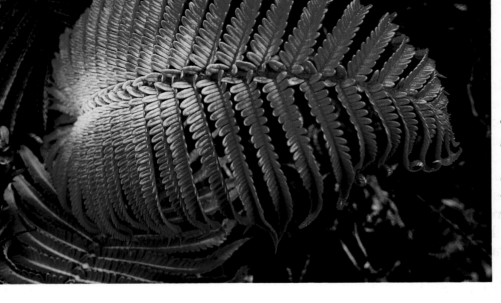

'Ama'u, *an endemic fern that ranges in height from 2 to 15 feet, grows in many different habitats but is most commonly seen in open, sunny areas around Kīlauea's summit caldera. Young 'ama'u fronds, typically red or salmon-colored when they unfurl, turn dark, glossy green as they mature.*

Sheltered from trade winds, the leeward slopes of Kīlauea and Mauna Loa lie in a "rain shadow" where yearly precipitation ranges from 20 to 60 inches. The effect of this rain shadow is obvious in the Ka'ū Desert, a sparsely vegetated area on the southwest side of Kīlauea's summit caldera. The Ka'ū Desert gets up to 50 inches of

The Ka'ū Desert, with Mauna Loa looming in the background, is characterized by sparse vegetation consisting of 'ōhi'a trees, scattered native shrubs ('ōhelo, pūkiawe, 'a'ali'i, and kūkaenēnē), and grasses (both native and alien). In spite of dry, harsh conditions, the Ka'ū Desert is also home to less obvious, rare plants, such as the Hawaiian catchfly, a small, wiry shrub. Because they resemble dead twigs, catchflies are often overlooked and trampled by unsuspecting hikers.

Volcanic fumes from a fissure eruption on Kīlauea's east rift zone inundated a forest of native ʻōhiʻa trees near Nāpau Crater in 1997. Mature ʻōhiʻa can apparently close openings in their leaves to exclude toxic gases, an adaptation that helps them survive exposure to sulfur dioxide released by the volcano. Many of these ʻōhiʻa lived, but trees nearer the active vent were killed by spatter falling from lava fountains and/or extreme heat and fumes.

rain each year—enough to support a forest—but the precipitation is a natural acid rain that inhibits plant growth. The rainfall in this region is acidic because it mixes with sulfur gases emitted from vents near Halemaʻumaʻu Crater. This part of the mid-elevation zone is also covered by 1790 ash, which has little capacity for retaining moisture. In spite of these conditions, scattered ʻōhelo, ʻaʻaliʻi, pūkiawe, and other native shrubs and grasses have adapted to life in the Kaʻū Desert.

Prevailing trade winds push moist air up the northeastern flanks of Kīlauea and Mauna Loa, and as the air rises, it cools and condenses, causing frequent and sometimes heavy rain on windward slopes. Most of the precipitation falls between 2,000 and 5,000 feet elevation, a region that includes the east side of Kīlauea's summit. As a result, lush rain forests have developed around Nāhuku and Kīlauea Iki, where annual rainfall often exceeds 100 inches.

ʻŌhiʻa dominates the uppermost canopy of most rain forests in Hawaiʻi Volcanoes. This abundant and widespread tree has adapted to nearly every ecological zone and is the most common tree in the park. In a few rain forests, koa emerges as the dominant or co-dominant tree of the high canopy. Secondary trees include ʻōlapa, kāwaʻu (Hawaiian holly), kōlea lau nui, pilo, and māmaki. The most conspicuous rain-forest plants are hāpuʻu. These tree ferns commonly reach heights of 20 feet and form a distinct layer beneath the ʻōhiʻa canopy. The greatest diversity of plants, however, occurs in the rain-forest understory, with more than 50 species of ferns and several native shrubs and herbs covering the forest floor.

On the higher slopes of Mauna Loa, park boundaries encompass three ecological zones: upland forests (4,000 to 6,700 feet), subalpine (6,700 to 9,000 feet), and alpine (9,000 feet to summit). Well-developed upland forests, characterized by koa, ʻōhiʻa, mānele (soapberry), ʻaʻaliʻi, and pūkiawe, exist in several kīpuka along the Mauna Loa Road. Scattered ʻōhiʻa, māmane, and native shrubs distinguish the subalpine zone from the alpine zone, where the harsh climate supports only sparse vegetation, primarily low shrubs with a few grasses, lichens, and mosses.

Come explore
with us

e how we
    present each
    subject in a
    colorful and
    entertaining way

e our *free*
    full-color catalog–

ll: 1-800-626-9673
    1-702-433-3415
x: 1-702-433-3420

sit our web site:
ww.kcpublications.com>

kc publications
THE STORY BEHIND THE SCENERY®

Mr.
Mrs.
Ms. _____
        First Name   *(Please Print)*   *Last Name*

Address _____

City _____ State/Province _____

Zip _____ Country _____

Day Phone _____

Fax _____ E-Mail _____

❑ Personal Use   ❑ Retail   ❑ Educational

Comments _____

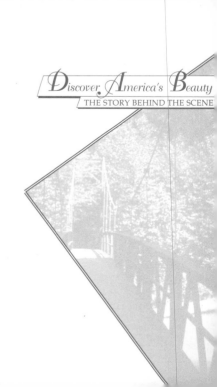

Discover America's Beauty
THE STORY BEHIND THE SCENE

Koa, *one of the largest native Hawaiian trees, grow up to 100 feet tall in ancient kīpuka on the Mauna Loa Road. Highly prized by Hawaiians for use as canoes, koa wood is still valued today for its beautiful finish on handcrafted products.*

NATIVE ANIMALS

Hawai'i's native land animals are limited to creatures that are small, mobile, and hardy enough to cross the Pacific Ocean naturally—mainly birds, insects, spiders, and snails. The only native land mammal is *'ōpe'ape'a*, the Hawaiian (hoary) bat, which roosts in trees and feeds on insects in park areas ranging from sea level to 10,000 feet elevation. There are no native amphibians or land reptiles on the islands.

Honu 'ea (hawksbill turtle), one of Hawai'i's indigenous marine reptiles, nests on sandy beaches within Hawai'i Volcanoes. The park actively manages the nesting sites of these endangered turtles to protect them and their eggs and hatchlings from being harmed or eaten by humans,

The endangered Hawaiian bat, 'ōpe'ape'a, roosts singly and is solitary except for a brief mating period. These small bats (3-5 inches long), which can be seen chasing insects at dusk, travel up to eight miles from their roosting sites in search of prey.

dogs, cats, birds, and mongooses. Hawai'i's only native marine mammal, the endangered monk seal, favors the northwestern islands of the Hawaiian Archipelago and is rarely seen along park shorelines.

More than 100 species of native birds—honeycreepers, seabirds, waterfowl, raptors, flightless birds, thrushes, and others—may have evolved from only 15 pioneer species on the islands. At least 50 of those species are now extinct, and nearly half of the surviving species are federally listed as threatened or endangered.

Hawaiian honeycreepers are the dominant bird group in Hawai'i's forests, although only 20 of the 45 species that evolved still exist—and of these, more than half are endangered. In Hawai'i Volcanoes, the native forest bird most likely to be seen and heard is a honeycreeper called *'apapane*. This crimson bird is abundant in forests along Kīlauea's Crater Rim Trail and in Kīpuka Puaulu. Other honeycreepers in the park include *common 'amakihi*, small yellowish-green birds that occupy a wide range of habitats, and *'i'iwi*, bright orange-red birds that are found mostly in upland

The majestic 'io, a native hawk favored by Hawaiian royalty, can sometimes be seen soaring gracefully over forests and grasslands in Hawai'i Volcanoes. Currently listed as an endangered species, 'io live only on the island of Hawai'i.

Revered as guardian spirits by early Hawaiians, pueo (native Hawaiian owls) are most commonly seen today hunting in grasslands, where they often hover before pouncing on prey. Active both day and night, pueo usually fly near the ground, but sometimes soar high overhead.

'Akiapōlā'au, once common in Hawai'i Volcanoes, are no longer found in the park. Small populations of this endangered honeycreeper still exist on Hawai'i Island, but they are at risk. 'Akiapōlā'au use their unusual bills to extract burrowing insects from trees—pecking at wood with stout, lower mandibles and prying prey from beneath bark with thin, upper ones.

forests and easily identified by their curved, salmon-colored bills.

When Polynesians first arrived, nine or more species of geese, at least seven of which were flightless, lived on the islands. These birds evolved in the absence of terrestrial predators, so they were easy prey for humans in search of food. As the human population boomed, hunting and loss of habitat drastically reduced the number of geese on the islands—to the point of extinction for all but one species. The surviving goose, the *nēnē*, is Hawai'i's state bird—and is a federally listed endangered species.

The population of *nēnē* on Hawai'i Island, which was estimated at 25,000 birds in the late 18th century, dwindled to as few as 30 birds by the early 1950s. Thanks to protective measures and captive breeding programs, the population is slowly increasing. Today, there are almost 400 *nēnē* on the island, nearly 40% of the total number that exist statewide. About 200 live within Hawai'i Volcanoes, where they can be seen searching for berries and grasses around Kīlauea caldera and on the slopes of Mauna Loa. At present, *nēnē* are still in peril—whether or not human efforts can save them from extinction remains to be seen.

Nēnē goslings remain with their parents until the next breeding season (about one year), learning how to forage for food and other life skills. Only about ten percent of nēnē nesting attempts in the wild result in surviving offspring. These two goslings, 4-6 weeks old, have beaten those odds, but their journey to adulthood is not guaranteed. A serious threat to their survival is poor nutrition—many nēnē goslings die from starvation due to the lack of high-protein vegetation in severely degraded habitats.

JACK JEFFREY

Munching a struggling fly, this Hawaiian caterpillar typifies the unique evolution on isolated islands. Only in Hawai'i are there caterpillars that ambush and eat living prey.

Native insects are abundant and widespread, having adapted to the full range of available habitats. Recent estimates suggest that nearly 10,000 endemic species evolved from just 350 to 400 colonizing insect species—an impressive example of evolution and adaptation! Most are small and well-camouflaged, so insects in Hawai'i Volcanoes are rarely noticed by park visitors.

Hawaiian spiders are generally elusive and not well-known, although more than 100 native species have been identified. Native land snails live on trees or the ground throughout the park, especially in damp areas—but, like Hawaiian insects, they are rather inconspicuous.

Hawaiian happyface spiders, with translucent bodies less than one-quarter inch long, are hard to see in the forest, where they live on the undersides of leaves. Why they display a wide variety of red and black patterns—including caricatures of human-like faces—on their backs is a puzzle. For now, we can only enjoy and marvel at them.

W. P. MULL

The small Indian mongoose was purposely introduced to Hawai'i in the late 1800s to control black rats in sugar cane fields. The experiment failed because mongooses sleep at night when rats are most active. Mongooses, which feed on eggs and young birds, are particularly devastating to Hawai'i's native ground-dwelling birds.

ALIEN INVADERS

Non-native species—plants and animals brought to Hawai'i by humans, either accidentally or on purpose—are called *alien* species. The term "introduced" is also used to identify non-native plants or animals. As soon as humans stepped ashore, alien plants and animals began invading the islands.

More than 30 plant species may have been introduced to Hawai'i by Polynesian settlers, who brought what they needed to establish life on a new island. When they set sail across the Pacific, the Polynesians carried *niu* (coconuts), *mai'a* (bananas), *'uala* (sweet potato), *kalo* (taro), and *kō* (sugar cane), which were planted as food crops. Most plants introduced by Polynesians had multiple uses. Early settlers used the *kī* (ti) plant for thatching houses, wrapping food, weaving sandals, making hula skirts, and in times of famine, for food. The oily nuts of *kukui* (candlenut) were burned for illumination or were roasted and eaten. *Kukui* flourished in lowland areas, and is now Hawai'i's state tree.

Polynesians also brought *pua'a* (pigs), *'īlio* (dogs), and *moa* (chickens) to the Hawaiian Islands as sources of food. They unwittingly transported geckos, skinks, Polynesian rats, and various insects and snails as accidental stowaways on their canoes. Of all the animals introduced by early settlers, Polynesian rats were probably the most invasive. They ate the eggs of ground-dwelling birds, fed on invertebrates, and destroyed plants, wreaking havoc on native species. Dogs and pigs were domesticated and kept close to settlements, so they probably caused little damage to the natural environment.

Beginning with the arrival of Captain Cook in 1778, the number and kinds of alien plants and animals on the islands increased dramatically. Cattle, goats, pigs, and sheep, which reached Hawai'i via European ships through the early 19th century, were especially destructive to native ecosystems. Free to roam the islands, these hoofed mammals established *feral* (domesticated animals gone wild) populations that ravaged native vegetation and spread alien plants through excretion of ingested seeds.

By the mid-1800s, the number of wild cattle on Hawai'i Island was estimated at 12,000. The goat population was probably five or six times larger. Today, cattle are confined to ranches and kept out of Hawai'i Volcanoes by fences. Feral goats have been eliminated from the park below 6,600 feet elevation, but a small number still roam higher, unfenced slopes of Mauna Loa.

Feral pigs continue to be agents of destruction in Hawai'i Volcanoes, particularly in rain forests, where they destroy habitat for native plants and animals, clearing the way for invasion of alien plants. While total eradication of feral pigs in the park might be the optimal solution to protect native plants and animals, it is not feasible. The next best solution is to build fences around specific areas in the park to keep feral pigs *out* of the forests. This method of environmental protection is expensive—a fence can cost up to $35,000 per mile to build—and is not possible in all areas of the park. To date, however, feral pigs have been removed from 25,000 acres of the park, and with fences installed to keep them pig-free, native rain forests are slowly recovering.

Alien plants and animals have invaded the islands throughout the 20th century, and despite preventive measures, they continue to spread today. Alien species compete for food and water, often displacing native species, and introduce or spread diseases to which native plants and animals have little natural immunity. Even alien insects such as yellowjackets, which probably reached the islands in a shipment of Christmas trees from the western United States, can disrupt an ecosystem by preying on larvae eaten by native birds and insects that pollinate native plants.

Like many areas on the island, Hawai'i Volcanoes is besieged by non-native species. Of the more than 600 alien plant species that have become established in the park, *kāhili ginger* and *faya tree* are two of the most abundant and widespread. First noticed in the park in 1961, faya trees have now invaded 30,000 acres of Hawai'i Volcanoes, where they are displacing 'ōhi'a and other native trees at an alarming rate.

More than half of the bird species found in the park are alien. Common mynas, northern cardinals, and Japanese white-eyes *(Mejiro)* were introduced to Hawai'i during the past 150 years. *Kalij pheasant*, commonly seen on park roads or trails in early morning or late afternoon, were released as gamebirds on a West Hawai'i ranch in 1962. Within 15 years, they invaded Hawai'i Volcanoes, where their numbers quickly increased.

Hawai'i now leads the United States in number of extinctions and federally listed endangered and threatened species. The loss of native species is attributed to habitat destruction and the invasion of alien species, both of which have been caused by humans. While it is too late to undo much of the damage, we can—with education and cooperation—prevent further degradation of Hawai'i's fragile environment and subsequent decline of native species. Hawai'i Volcanoes National Park, established to protect and preserve natural and cultural resources, is a step toward that goal.

JACK JEFFREY

Feral pigs dig up soil searching for earthworms and slugs, and eat or trample every native plant in their path. They knock over tree ferns to eat the starchy interior of the trunks, and in doing so, create places where water accumulates. This water allows the breeding of mosquitoes (non-native insects), which transmit alien avian diseases that are harmful to native birds. The destructive activity of feral pigs is, therefore, indirectly responsible for the demise of Hawai'i's native birds.

SUGGESTED READING

HAWAII AUDUBON SOCIETY. *Hawaii's Birds.* Honolulu: Hawaii Audubon Society, 1993 (revised edition).

HOWARTH, FRANCIS G., and WILLIAM P. MULL. *Hawaiian Insects and Their Kin.* Honolulu: University of Hawai'i Press, 1992.

KAY, E. ALISON (editor). *A Natural History of the Hawaiian Islands, Selected Readings II.* Honolulu: University of Hawai'i Press, 1994.

LAMOUREUX, CHARLES H. *Trailside Plants of Hawai'i's National Parks.* Hawai'i National Park: Hawai'i Natural History Association, 1996 (revised edition).

RASP, RICHARD A. *in pictures Hawai'i Volcanoes: The Continuing Story.* Las Vegas, Nevada: KC Publications, 1992.

STONE, CHARLES P., and LINDA W. PRATT. *Hawai'i's Plants and Animals: Biological Sketches of Hawai'i Volcanoes National Park.* Hawai'i National Park: Hawai'i Natural History Association, 1994.

PHILIP ROSENBERG

Kāhili ginger was intentionally planted around park housing 50 years ago—before the detrimental effects of introduced plants were recognized—and quickly spread to other areas. Today, kāhili ginger almost dominates the ground cover in some parts of Kīlauea's rain forests.

Those Who Came Before...

About 1,600 years ago, intrepid voyagers from the Marquesas Islands set sail from their homeland in the South Pacific and headed north. Using the sun, stars, ocean currents, and seabirds as guides, they navigated their double-hulled canoes, rigged with huge, triangular sails made of woven *pandanus* leaves, across more than 2,000 miles of open sea. Why they left the Marquesas is not known—perhaps they were defeated in war or driven away by drought and famine—but archaeologists believe that these seafaring Polynesians were the first people to discover and colonize the Hawaiian Islands.

Hawaiian *mo'olelo* (historical stories) also speak of a second migration to Hawai'i about 800 years ago by Polynesians from *Kahiki*, generally believed to be Tahiti in the Society Islands. According to legend, these skilled navigators sailed back and forth between the two island groups for the next few centuries, bringing more people and new ideas to Hawai'i. The Polynesians who settled in Hawai'i gradually diverged from their ancestral roots in the Marquesas and Society Islands, and developed a complex and sophisticated culture that is uniquely Hawaiian.

As this society emerged, it became highly stratified. *Ali'i*, the highest class, were thought to be direct descendants of the *akua* (gods), and as such, were considered sacred. The *ali'i nui* (high chief) ruled over the island, which was divided into *moku* (districts) governed by lesser chiefs. *Moku* were subdivided into *ahupua'a*, wedge-shaped sections of land that extended from the mountains to the sea. The tenants of each *ahupua'a* had access to a variety of natural resources—from *lā'au* (trees) in upland forests to *i'a* (fish) in the ocean—and were essentially self-sufficient.

Maka'āinana, the largest class, were commoners—farmers, fishermen, craftsmen, and warriors—who lived and worked on the land. Every family in an *ahupua'a* performed specific duties, such as planting crops, building canoes, or weaving *lau hala* mats, under the direction of the *konohiki* (land manager). Each year, *maka'āinana* paid taxes—tributes of food and handcrafted products—to the *ali'i* during *makahiki*, a four-month festival around the time of fall harvest. Although *maka'āinana* were free to move to other *ahupua'a*, many families remained on the same land for generations.

Whether they were *ali'i* or *maka'āinana*, the behavior of early Hawaiians was regulated by an elaborate *kapu* (taboo) system. *Kapu* defined the relationship between classes and dictated what people could and could not do. For instance, men and women were not allowed to eat together, and women were forbidden from eating foods associated with the *akua*, such as pork, coconuts, certain

Ki'i pōhaku, *Hawaiian petroglyphs, are generally found along trails or near ancient land boundaries and usually occur in groups rather than as single units. In Hawai'i Volcanoes, thousands of petroglyphs—many of which may be related to birth and life—cover Pu'u Loa and the surrounding area.*

JACK JEFFREY

After weeks of sailing, the appearance of shorebirds and clouds surrounding a high mountain peak gave hope to Polynesian voyagers that land was near. Any doubts that double-hulled canoes—navigated by the sun, stars, and ocean currents, and powered with sails of woven pandanus leaves—could successfully cross the Pacific were put to rest in 1976 when the Hokule'a, a 60-foot replica of an ancient voyaging canoe, sailed from Hawai'i to Tahiti and back without modern navigation instruments. Herb Kawainui Kāne, general designer and builder of the Hokule'a and captain of its training crew, created this painting.

fish, and some varieties of bananas. *Maka'āinana* were required to kneel or lay face down in the presence of *ali'i*. *Kapu* also controlled when and how natural resources in the *ahupua'a* were used. *Kapu* were strictly obeyed—failure to do so resulted in severe punishment, often death.

The daily activities of early Hawaiians were strongly influenced by their belief in the sacred powers of four major gods—*Kāne, Kū, Lono,* and *Kanaloa*—and innumerable minor gods and goddesses. To honor these *akua*, the people built *heiau*, places of worship, which ranged from massive, rock-walled temples to small shrines consisting of a single upright stone. Every signif-

icant event, from giving birth to building a house, required some kind of religious ritual, prayer, or offering at the *heiau* to ensure that the endeavor was successful. At *heiau* built for Lono, the god of agriculture, prayers for rain and abundant crops were accompanied by offerings of bananas, coconuts, and pigs. Neglecting the *akua*, it was believed, would invoke their anger and result in dire consequences.

The largest and most elaborate *heiau* were *luakini*, temples where human sacrifices took place, which were dedicated to *Kū*, the god of war. Waha'ula Heiau (temple of the red mouth), on Kīlauea's south coast, is believed to have

In July 1997, lava buried Waha'ula Heiau, a temple complex that once consisted of at least five structures defined by rock walls up to six feet thick and six feet high. Red cinder embedded in the walls may have been symbolic of luakini *rituals (human sacrifices) conducted at Waha'ula. In 1989, flows destroyed the park visitor center at this site (ruins in background), and on five different occasions, lava came into contact with heiau structures—but did not bury them. Eight years later, molten rock entombed Waha'ula Heiau and engulfed what was left of the visitor center.*

been the first *luakini* in the Hawaiian Islands. Built by Pa'ao, a priest from Kahiki, around 1275 A.D., the *heiau* was used for more than five centuries. Rituals at Waha'ula, the last *luakini* on the island of Hawai'i to be abandoned, ceased in 1819. The *heiau* ruins narrowly escaped being buried by lava in 1989. Eight years later, lava flows inundated the site once again—and Waha'ula is now preserved forever beneath more than 50 feet of volcanic rock.

PELE, THE GODDESS

Of the many demigods held sacred by early Hawaiians, Pele, the goddess of volcanoes, may have had the most profound effect on their lives. According to legend, Pele came to Hawai'i from Kahiki seeking a new home for her fires and her family. She traveled south from Ni'ihau to Maui, digging fire pits on each island along the way, but none were suitable, so she moved on. When Pele reached the island of Hawai'i, she finally found the ideal conditions for her fires in Halema'uma'u Crater at the summit of Kīlauea Volcano, which is still recognized as her home today.

In the years since the first settlers arrived on Hawai'i Island, nearly every square foot of Kīlauea has been covered by new lava flows, so it is no wonder that early Hawaiians revered Pele and feared her wrath. Many stories tell of her fiery vengeance on people who failed to pay her proper respect, so native Hawaiians regularly

According to legend, when Pele reached Hawai'i, she found 'Ailā'au, a fire god, living on Kīlauea. Pele wanted the volcano for her new home, so she and 'Ailā'au fought, each throwing fireballs, shaking the earth, and sending lava flows across the land in a furious battle. When the smoke finally cleared, 'Ailā'au was gone—and because she had beaten him, Pele was respected as goddess of the volcano by the people of Hawai'i. Today, she is still honored with offerings of song, chant, and dance at her home in Halema'uma'u Crater. In this Herb Kāne painting of Pele, the reflection of "fire" can be seen in her eyes.

paid tribute to Pele with rituals of *oli* (chant), *mele* (song), and *hula* (dance), and appeased her with special gifts of black pigs, red fish, and select native plants. (Contrary to popular belief, young virgins were never sacrificed to the goddess.) The spirit of Pele continues to live in the hearts and minds of many native Hawaiians, some of whom still offer *ho'okupu* (tributes) or honor her with *hula* and *oli* at the edge of Halema'uma'u Crater.

COASTAL SETTLEMENTS

Driving down the Chain of Craters Road in Hawai'i Volcanoes today, you may find it hard to believe that thousands of people once lived on the south flank of Kīlauea—but they did. The boundaries of more than a dozen *ahupua'a* have been identified, and remnants of villages and settlement sites, many of which were occupied until the late 1800s, are scattered along the coastal plain and park lowlands. Thousands of *ki'i pōhaku* (petroglyphs) have been found on the volcanic rock in this region. These rock carvings may record significant events in the lives of the early Hawaiians, but their actual meanings are a matter of conjecture among archaeologists.

Kīlauea's early residents cultivated sweet potato, taro, sugar cane, and other dryland crops in the rocky terrain, and raised pigs, chickens, and

Each year, an investiture of Hawai'i Island's Royal Court, which portrays ali'i (royalty) of ancient times, is held at the rim of Halema'uma'u Crater on Kīlauea Volcano. This is just one of many special events that take place during Aloha Festivals, a statewide celebration perpetuating Hawaiian customs and traditions. The investiture ceremony, depicting the color, splendor, and ritual of old Hawai'i, is accompanied by oli *(chants) and* hula *(dance). Dancers wearing traditional* pā'ū hula *(dance skirts) made from* hau, *and* lei *(head and neck ornaments) made of* palapalai, *honor the Royal Court with hula that venerates the goddess Pele. After their performance, the dancers toss their lei into the crater as* ho'okupu *(tribute) to Pele. These heartfelt expressions are reminders that the Hawaiian culture is very much alive.*

'Ōhelo, *a native shrub related to cranberries, is known for its edible berries—a favorite of humans and, according to legend, the Hawaiian goddess Pele. To prevent overcollection of* 'ōhelo, *a source of food for endangered* nēnē, *restrictions have been placed on picking berries in the park.*

The fruits of 'ōlapa *are eaten by native forest birds. In gentle breezes, the leaves of this tree flutter and sway in graceful motions characteristic of hula. For this reason, dancers often look to* 'ōlapa *for inspiration.*

dogs for food. Men fished in the deep coastal waters, while women harvested shellfish, seaweed, and salt along the rugged shoreline. Children were cared for and taught by their *kūpuna* (grandparents). Where freshwater was scarce, people used calabashes to collect drips of water seeping through the rock in lava tubes. They ventured into the upland forests to log huge *koa* trees for building canoes and to gather colorful bird feathers for the royal capes of the *ali'i*. They traveled on an extensive trail system to visit their extended families in other districts, and trekked to the summit of the volcano to pay homage to Pele. Their lives were occasionally challenged by droughts, hurricanes, tsunami, earthquakes, and volcanic eruptions, but they persevered. And every day, as they worked and played, they prayed to their *'aumakua* (guardian spirit) and other *akua* for guidance and protection.

With the arrival of European ships in the late 18th century, foreign ideas and goods pervaded the Hawaiian culture, and introduced diseases began taking a toll on the indigenous population. Remote villages, like those in Hawai'i Volcanoes, were the least affected by these changes—for a while. By the mid-1800s, however, a series of political and economic events—the death of King Kamehameha, the abolishment of the *kapu* system, the arrival of missionaries, and the *Māhele* (legislation allowing ownership of land)—completely changed the fabric of early Hawaiian society, which affected the lives of all native people on the island, even in remote areas. The final blow to Kīlauea's coastal settlements came in 1868, when a huge earthquake (estimated magnitude 7.9) and subsequent tsunami destroyed most of the villages. Instead of rebuilding their homes, many of the survivors moved to Hilo or other towns, bringing an end to their traditional Hawaiian lifestyle.

SUGGESTED READING

Cox, J. Halley, and Edward Stasack. *Hawaiian Petroglyphs.* Honolulu: Bishop Museum Press, 1970.

Culliney, John L. *Islands in a Far Sea (Nature and Man in Hawaii).* San Francisco: Sierra Club Books, 1988.

Daws, Gavan. *Shoal of Time (A History of the Hawaiian Islands).* Honolulu: University of Hawai'i Press, 1968.

Kāne, Herb K. *Pele, Goddess of Hawai'i's Volcanoes.* Captain Cook, Hawai'i: The Kawainui Press, 1987.

Kirch, Patrick V. *Feathered Gods and Fishhooks (An Introduction to Hawaiian Archaeology and Prehistory).* Honolulu: University of Hawai'i Press, 1985.

Creating A Park

Sixteen years after Captain Cook discovered the Hawaiian Islands, Archibald Menzies, a Scottish naturalist, ascended the slopes of Mauna Loa, becoming the first European to venture into what is now Hawai'i Volcanoes National Park. Kīlauea was not visited by Western explorers until nearly 30 years later when in 1823, an English missionary named William Ellis and three American colleagues became the first non-Hawaiians to enter the sacred domain of Pele.

Much of what we know about early 19th-century Hawai'i is from Ellis's written account of his excursion around the island. In addition to providing invaluable information about the lives and customs of native Hawaiians living on Kīlauea, his journal includes detailed descriptions and captivating narratives about the volcano.

> *. . . we at length came to the edge of the great crater, where a spectacle, sublime and even appalling, presented itself before us—We stopped, and trembled. Astonishment and awe for some moments rendered us mute, and, like statues, we stood fixed to the spot, with our eyes riveted on the abyss below.*
> —from JOURNAL OF WILLIAM ELLIS

When Ellis's journal and other vivid accounts of Hawai'i's active volcano were published in newspapers around the world, Kīlauea quickly became a popular destination for adventurous travelers.

In the mid-1800s, the two-day trip to Kīlauea's summit was not easy. Depending on the route taken, it was either a bone-jarring trek over rough fields of volcanic rock from the coast at Keauhou or Punalu'u, or a soggy ride through the rain forest from Hilo. Accommodations at the top of Kīlauea were little more than thatched huts until a permanent structure, the first Volcano House, was constructed in 1866. During the next 75 years, the hotel was remodeled or rebuilt

G. BRAD LEWIS

"... The camera cannot measure its depths, convey its sounds, or depict its glow. Those and only those who have looked into its depths, heard its roar or felt its burning heat can ever know the power, the wonder, the magic of the spell it casts upon one." These words, recorded in the Volcano House Register by Frances King Headler in 1909, were written about Halema'uma'u, but aptly describe the churning lake of lava in Pu'u 'Ō'ō crater nearly nine decades later.

several times. The 1877 structure survived and now houses the Volcano Art Center gallery. The most recent Volcano House, the only hotel in the park today, was built in 1941.

Volcano House guests were encouraged to write about their experiences on Kīlauea in the hotel register—a tradition that continued until the mid-1900s. Their comments and observations, which range from humorous to poetic to profound, document Kīlauea's volcanic activity for more than 90 years. For this reason, the

Volcano House Register is an important source of information for scientists studying the history of the volcano.

Alteration of Hawai'i's native ecosystems had begun with the arrival of the first Polynesians, who cut lowland forests to clear land for agriculture and burned grasslands to encourage the growth of *pili*, a grass used for thatching. When Westerners arrived, their steel axes and introduced animals—goats and cattle—were even more effective than Polynesian stone

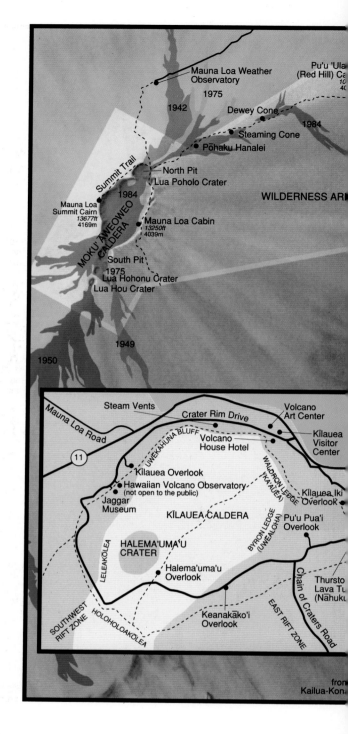

A park ranger-interpreter explains how plants become established on new lava flows. During guided walks, such as this one into Kīlauea Iki, visitors learn about the geologic, biologic, and cultural resources in Hawai'i Volcanoes.

adzes in destroying native forests. As degradation of the environment continued, the need to protect Kīlauea's natural beauty and resources became apparent, and the idea for a national park was born.

In 1906, Lorrin Thurston, publisher of two Honolulu newspapers, launched a campaign to establish Kīlauea National Park, but he was not immediately successful. In 1912, Dr. Thomas Jaggar, the founder of the Hawaiian Volcano Observatory, joined the campaign, and together they lobbied for support, writing editorials and escorting Congressional delegates on trips through the proposed park lands. Four years later, their efforts paid off. On August 1, 1916, President Woodrow Wilson signed the bill creating our 12th national park.

Hawai'i National Park, as it was then called, originally included the summits of Kīlauea and Mauna Loa on the island of Hawai'i and Haleakalā Volcano on the island of Maui. Over the years, additional land was purchased, exchanged, and donated to the park, extending the boundaries to include the Ka'ū and Kalapana regions on Kīlauea and the Ola'a tract on Mauna Loa. In 1961, Haleakalā became a separate national park—the section on Hawai'i Island was renamed Hawai'i Volcanoes National Park.

Hawai'i Volcanoes, a patchwork of stark, black volcanic rock and lush, green tropical forests, now includes almost 230,000 acres of land, half of which is wilderness. About 2.5 million

people from around the world visit the park each year to witness its active volcanoes, explore its unique and complex ecosystems, and learn about the distinct Hawaiian culture. In recognition of its outstanding geologic, biologic, and cultural values, Hawai'i Volcanoes was designated an International Biosphere Reserve in 1980 and a World Heritage Site in 1987.

HAWAI'I VOLCANOES TODAY

Every national park seeks to preserve the natural and cultural resources of the land encompassed by its boundaries. But in Hawai'i Volcanoes, where volcanic eruptions can alter the landscape in a matter of hours, preservation takes on greater urgency.

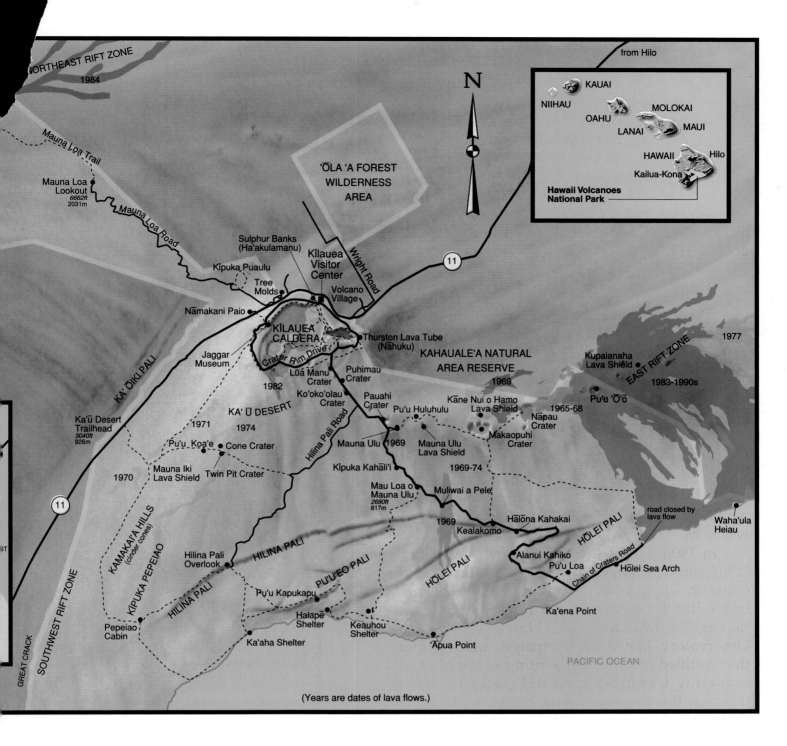

Years have been devoted to mapping and recording archaeological sites in Hawai'i Volcanoes, but due to the high density of features and the enormous area to be surveyed, only two percent of the park has been inventoried. Of the approximately 31,000 documented archaeological features, about half have been covered by lava since 1983. Pu'u Loa, the largest concentration of petroglyphs in the park, and countless other features are still under threat from the ongoing eruption. Park archaeologists are striving to document the remains of Kīlauea's rich cultural heritage before the stories that they can tell us are silenced forever.

Active lava flows are part of the natural environment in Hawai'i Volcanoes—a cycle of destruction and creation that cannot be controlled by humans. On the other hand, the introduction of alien plants and animals and the loss of native species are unnatural changes that can be

(Text continues on page 48.)

SUGGESTED READING

BEVENS, DARCY (editor). *On the Rim of Kīlauea (Excerpts from the Volcano House Register)*. Hawai'i National Park: Hawai'i Natural History Association, 1992.

WRIGHT, THOMAS L., TAEKO JANE TAKAHASHI, and J. D. GRIGGS. *Hawai'i Volcano Watch*. Honolulu: University of Hawai'i Press, 1992.

prevented or minimized. To protect and perpetuate native ecosystems in Hawai'i Volcanoes, biologically diverse and relatively intact sections of the park called Special Ecological Areas are being intensively managed to eradicate alien plants. To preserve habitat for native species, park managers are also fostering partnerships with managers of adjacent lands.

In Hawai'i Volcanoes, the land, its resources, and the Hawaiian culture are very much alive and interconnected. Walking along ancient coastal trails, you can feel the presence of the early Hawaiians who lived on the slopes of Kīlauea. Watching red-hot, molten lava wend its way down the volcanic slopes and pour into the ocean, you sense the awesome power of the earth and your own insignificance in the grand scheme of life.

The overwhelming nature of Hawai'i Volcanoes can render you almost speechless, as it did H. T. Collins, a park visitor, in 1920. After seeing Kīlauea's crater of seething lava, his only comment in the Volcano House Register is a classic understatement—"Nuthin' like it in Oklahoma."

G. BRAD LEWIS

Lava flowing into the ocean explodes in a fiery display.

Books on National Park areas in "The Story Behind the Scenery" series are: Acadia, Alcatraz Island, Arches, Badlands, Big Bend, Biscayne, Blue Ridge Parkway, Bryce Canyon, Canyon de Chelly, Canyonlands, Cape Cod, Capitol Reef, Channel Islands, Civil War Parks, Colonial, Crater Lake, Death Valley, Denali, Devils Tower, Dinosaur, Everglades, Fort Clatsop, Gettysburg, Glacier, Glen Canyon-Lake Powell, Grand Canyon, Grand Canyon-North Rim, Grand Teton, Great Basin, Great Smoky Mountains, Haleakalā, Hawai'i Volcanoes, Independence, Jewel Cave, Joshua Tree, Lake Mead & Hoover Dam, Lassen Volcanic, Lincoln Parks, Mammoth Cave, Mesa Verde, Mount Rainier, Mount Rushmore, National Park Service, National Seashores, North Cascades, Olympic, Petrified Forest, Rainbow Bridge, Redwood, Rocky Mountain, Scotty's Castle, Sequoia & Kings Canyon, Shenandoah, Statue of Liberty, Theodore Roosevelt, Virgin Islands, Wind Cave, Yellowstone, Yosemite, Zion.

A companion series on National Park areas is the *"in pictures...The Continuing Story."* This series has **Translation Packages**, providing each title with a complete text both in English and, individually, a second language, German, French, or Japanese. Selected titles in both this series and our other books are available in up to 8 languages.

NEW! WildLife @ Yellowstone.

Additional books in "The Story Behind the Scenery" series are: Annapolis, Big Sur, California Gold Country, California Trail, Colorado Plateau, Columbia River Gorge, Fire: A Force of Nature, Grand Circle Adventure, John Wesley Powell, Kaua'i, Lake Tahoe, Las Vegas, Lewis & Clark, Monument Valley, Mormon Temple Square, Mormon Trail, Mount St. Helens, Nevada's Red Rock Canyon, Nevada's Valley of Fire, Oregon Trail, Oregon Trail Center, Pony Express, Santa Catalina, Santa Fe Trail, Sharks, Sonoran Desert, U.S. Virgin Islands, Water: A Gift of Nature, Whales & Dolphins.

To receive our catalog with over 115 titles:

Call (800-626-9673), fax (702-433-3420), write to the address below, Or visit our web site at www.kcpublications.com

Published by KC Publications, 3245 E. Patrick Ln., Suite A, Las Vegas, NV 89120.

Inside back cover: Re-enactment of Chiefess Kapi'olani defying Pele at Halema'uma'u in 1824. Photo by Peter French.

Back cover: Sunrise illuminates new land on Kīlauea's actively growing coastline. Photo by Clint Farlinger.

Created, Designed, and Published in the U.S.A.
Ink formulated by Daihan Ink Co., Ltd.
Printed by Doosan Dong-A Co., Ltd., Seoul, Korea
Color Separations by Kedia/Kwang Yang Sa Co., Ltd.
Paper produced exclusively by Hankuk Paper Mfg. Co., Ltd.